DEDICATION

To all our family and friends— your unwavering support and encouragement inspired us to dream big and persevere through the journey of creating our very first book as best friends and collaborators.

To Deborah, Marcy, Nejla, and Robin, for guiding us through the publishing process and helping us bring this dream to life.

In the heart of Asmara, four best friends are crazy about basketball. Too young for the local gym court, they dare to dream bigger — building one of their own! With unstoppable energy and bold fundraising ideas, they set out to make it happen. But can their determination turn a dream into reality?

The Eri Basketball Boys

By Jonah Seyum, Hiyab Yosief, and Kudus Robel

"Ugh!" said Senay. "We still don't have a basketball court
to play on."
"I wish we could build one on that empty lot my dad has,"
 said Kudus.
 "We don't have enough money for that; we'll just have to play
on a court around here," said Hiyab.
"And besides, we don't have a good basketball or shoes
either,"added Jonah.

"Let's try Bocciofila Asmara (Bo-tcho-Feel-ee-a)," said
Senay. "We have just enough money to play." They
arrived and knocked on the door.

The assistant referee laughed. "You guys are too
young; you won't play well enough for the adults. Just
play in the canchello."

"The canchello is too small, and there's no hoop,"
said Jonah. "And we can pay to play here."
The ref shrugged and closed the door to Bocciofila.

CLUB BOCCIOFILA ASMARA

The friends dragged themselves over to the canchello. They threw the ball over the gate as a basket.

It was so hard to score, and they had to worry about passing cars in the neighborhood.

"Man, I wish we had our own court," said Hiyab.

"Let's at least get a better ball," said Kudus.

The next day, they collected their money and walked to the shop. There it was—a beautiful basketball! They raced into the shop to buy it, but—

"Wait! The assistant ref from Bocciofila is trying to get the last basketball!" Jonah yelled.

The boys sprinted to get the last basketball before he did—

But the ref had already bought it.

Supermarket

"Sorry to bother you, sir, but we need that ball because we don't have good basketballs," said Jonah.
"Well, we need this ball because ours are very deflated," the ref said.

"Let's make a deal," said Jonah. "If you give us that ball, we will never bug you at Bocciofila ever again."

"Alright, deal," said the ref. He gave the boys the ball. "I better never see you again," he said, and walked right back to Bocciofila.

"Now we need a court," said Kudus. "My dad said we could build one on that empty lot...if we can pay for it."

"Huh? We could barely afford to play at Bocciofila, and now we build an outdoor court!?" said Senay.

"We can raise money," said Hiyab.
"How? We only have 300 Nakfa!" said Kudus.
"We could sell chocolate or something like that," said Senay.

"We can wash cars for people in the neighborhood!" said Hiyab, getting excited.

"Does anyone know how much an outdoor court costs?"
"It costs about $1000, which is 15,000 Nakfa!" said Kudus.

The friends worked every day to get sales, but nothing worked.
"We need a better plan," said Jonah. "Let's hand out fliers."

Then, one day, finally, they got their first car wash
customer. Then another. And another.

Each boy took chocolates to his own neighborhood and worked to make money however he could.

Every week, they counted how much they had made. As the hours, days, weeks, and months passed, their collection grew.

"Yes! We finally got 10,000 Nakfa from our businesses,"
said Jonah. "We still need 5,000 Nakfa to build the court."

They kept working hard and finally reached 14,000 Nakfa.
Jonah's mom said, "We can give you 2,000 Nakfa under one
condition: You let other kids in the neighborhood come and
play with you."

"Deal," said the boys.

The workers came to build the court. The boys were extra happy—their dream was coming true! "Let's make our floor blue, red, and green," Kudus said.

"Yeah! Our court name can be ERI STAR," added Hiyab.

But when Kudus and Senay told the workers that they would like "ERI STAR" on the court, the man said, "Ah, it will cost 2,000 more Nakfa to make a custom ERI STAR logo."

Yikes! The boys worked so hard to get this far, and now they needed more money to make a logo for the court. Senay reported the news to Jonah and Hiyab. "What! How are we supposed to get 2,000 more Nakfa?" yelled Jonah.

The friends picked up their wash rags and chocolates and hit their neighborhoods again. It took another two weeks to collect the 2,000 Nakfa needed for the logo, longer than they expected.

Finally, the court was ready.

"Why don't we have a huge party on the court for everyone?" Senay suggested.

"Good idea! We could have food, drinks, and invite the whole neighborhood," added Jonah.

"We could have a dunk contest and shooting 3-pointers contest!" said Kudus excitedly.

"Don't forget the jamming music!" said Hiyab.

The boys' parents agreed to help with food, drinks, and decorations. Hiyab's brother agreed to DJ. They invited everyone to the grand opening.

The day of the party came. Everyone met at Hiyab's house. "Okay, tablecloth—check. DJ? Check. Invitations? Check..." Jonah went on. "We've got everything. Let's go!" They were so excited to finally have a court in their backyard and play whenever they wanted to—one that they worked for—and could share with everyone in the neighborhood, not just people who had money, like Bocciofila.

The first guests arrived at the party. "Woah! Guys, this is amazing!" said one girl.
"This is epic!" said their friend Nathan.

The food was kickin' and the DJ was fire! Everyone felt connected to the court, because they had brought food or drinks, had their car washed, or donated to help this court exist. The boys got their basketball court, and everyone was happy.

As the party ended, a group of neighbors presented the boys with a gift. "Thank you for making our community better," they said. "We want to do something nice for you." The boys opened the package to find four sets of basketball shoes.

Jonah, Hiyab, Kudus and Senay put on their new shoes and gathered on their special logo. Together, they shouted, "On the count of three... 3-2-1—Eri basketball boys for life!"

1. Location: Eritrea is a country in East Africa with a rich history and unique cultural traits. Eritrea is located in the Horn of Africa. Eritrea is home to one of the oldest port cities in Africa and is an African destination that many people dream of visiting.

2. Currency: Nakfa is the currency of Eritrea. 1 dollar = 15 Nakfa

3. Diverse Languages: Eritrea is home to nine official languages, including Tigrinya, Tigre, and Arabic. While most people speak Tigrinya, the country is a melting pot of different linguistic and cultural groups.

4. Geography: Eritrea has a stunning diversity in landscapes, from the mountainous highlands to the coastal plains along the Red Sea. It also has several islands, including the Dahlak Archipelago, known for its beautiful coral reefs and marine life.

5. Asmera: The capital city, Asmera (also spelled Asmara), is known for its well-preserved colonial Italian architecture. The city has been recognized as a UNESCO World Heritage Site because of its unique blend of modernist and Art Deco styles, which is rare in Africa.

6. Coffee: Like Ethiopia, Eritrea has a deep coffee culture. Coffee ceremonies are an important part of social life, with people gathering to roast and brew coffee beans, which are often grown locally.

7. National Independence: Eritrea gained independence from Ethiopia after a 30-year-long war, finally achieving sovereignty in 1993. This struggle for independence is still a key element of national identity today.

8. No Fast-Food Chains: Eritrea is one of the few countries in the world where major global fast-food chains like McDonald's or KFC are not present. Instead, local eateries offer traditional Eritrean dishes.

9. Eritrean Cuisine: The cuisine features a lot of stews, lentils, and vegetables. A famous dish is Shiro, a flavorful chickpea-based stew, injera (a spongy flatbread), kuluwa/zigni (a spicy stew), and so much more.

10. Red Sea Access: Eritrea has a coastline along the Red Sea, making it strategically important for trade. The country is also known for its pristine beaches and rich marine life, which have become a growing tourist attraction.

Jonah Seyum, a 12-year-old globe-trotter, has visited 22 countries with his mom and achieved the remarkable feat of publishing six best-selling books. He has a passion for travel and cherishes spending time with his family—especially his parents and his 30 cousins, who are spread across Minneapolis, Atlanta, Orlando, Denver, and Eritrea. Beyond his love for adventure, Jonah enjoys playing basketball with friends, performing on his violin, and diving into epic Fortnite battles on his PS4. He has a strong affinity for math and history, enjoys learning new languages, and finds joy in listening to music.

Hiyab Yosief, a 15-year-old resident of Asmara, Eritrea, is thrilled to see his name on a published book for the very first time. Alongside this new milestone, he has also translated several English books into Tigrinya, the language of Eritrea. Hiyab enjoys playing basketball and cherishing moments with friends. In his free time, he enjoys gaming—especially NBA 2K—at local video game spots in Asmara. He is a tech enthusiast, he stays up-to-date with the latest technologies, using them to excel in school and stay connected with family and friends across the world.

Kudus Robel, a 12-year-old from the vibrant city of Asmara, Eritrea, is ecstatic to celebrate the publication of his very first book. A passionate reader, he treasures quality time with friends through gaming and eagerly embraces new hobbies. Kudus holds a special fondness for the tradition of Sunday coffee ceremonies with his family. He also enjoys road trips with his siblings, especially to Massawa, Eritrea (Red Sea), where he delights in swimming and savoring fresh fish. Looking ahead, Kudus dreams of becoming both an NBA player and a computer engineer.